To Panda and Duffy
our favorite furry little kids
 SGT & JRE

To the littlest kid with the big kick
 M.A.F.

A Preschool Read·A·Picture Book™
Little Kids at Play

Written by Jeffie Ross Gordon
Illustrated by Mary Ann Fraser

MODERN PUBLISHING
A Division of Unisystems, Inc.
New York, NY 10022

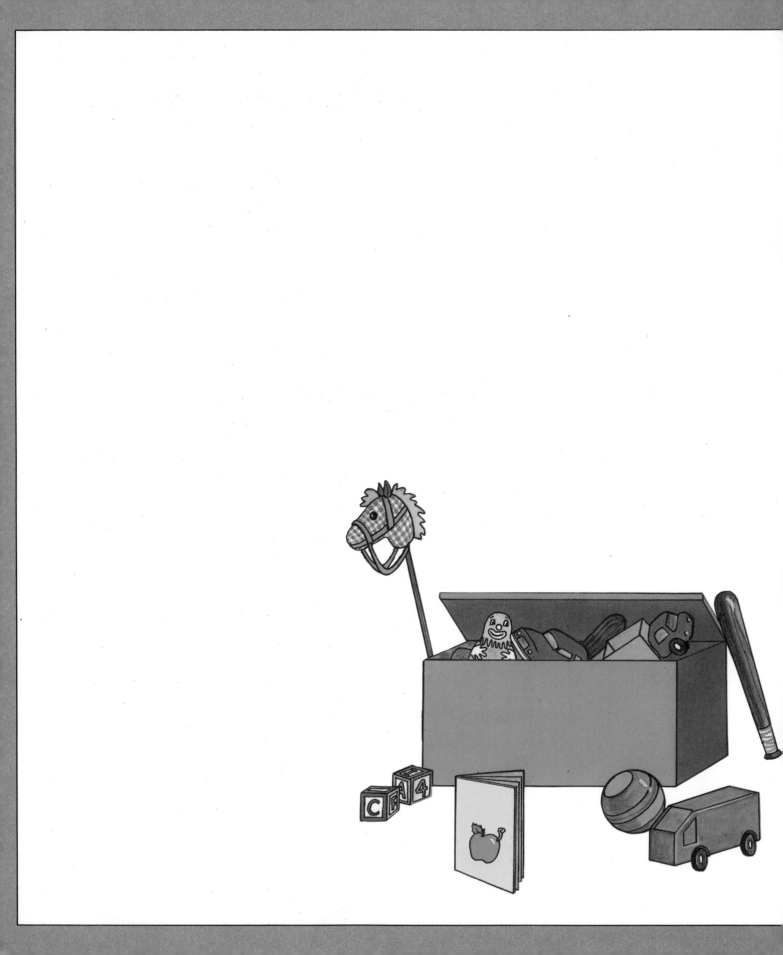

Table of Contents

Say Please

Words for Say Please

 Emmy

 ice cream cone

 Ethan

hand

 Pooch

Say Please

 had an  .

"  ," said her little brother,  . He held out his  .

The  dripped.

 , the dog, licked up the drips.

"I want an  ," said  .

"Say please," said  , as she put the  behind her back to tease  .

 snuck up behind her and ate the  .

"Okay," said  . "Please."

 then handed  the  . The ice cream was missing.

"I want my  and  ate it," said  .

"  , don't you know you have to say please?" asked  .

Sharing

New words for Sharing

 cars

 house

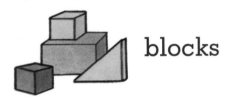 blocks

Words you have learned

 Ethan

 Emmy

Sharing

was playing with his 🚗 .

was playing with her 🧱 . She built a 🏠 of 🧱 .

"May I use one of your 🚗 ?" asked 👧 .

"No," said 👦 . He bumped his 🚗 into the 🏠 of 🧱 . The 🏠 of 🧱 fell down.

"That was not nice," said 👧 . She built another 🏠 of 🧱 . 👦 bumped the new 🏠 of 🧱 .

"That was not nice, 👦 ," said 👧 again. She picked up the 🧱 and began to build. "Now there is a 🏠 of 🧱 for me and a 🏠 of 🧱 for you," said 👧 .

"Thank you," said 👦 . He put his little 🚗 into his 🏠 of 🧱 . Then he took one of the 🚗 out and gave it to 👧 .

"Thank you," said 👧 . "Now we can play 🚗 and 🧱 together."

He's My Brother

New words for He's My Brother

 bear

 tree

Words you have learned

 Emmy

 cars

 Ethan

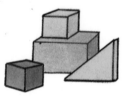 blocks

He's My Brother

(girl) and her friend Jane were playing.

"Let's pretend I'm a (bear)," said Jane. "Grr. Grr. We can climb a

(tree) and look for honey."

"I want to play. I'm a (bear) too," said (boy). "Grr. Grr."

"(boy), you're too little to play with us," said Jane.

"You can play with (car) and (blocks)," said (girl).

"I want to be a (bear)," said (boy).

"We don't need another (bear)," said Jane.

"But we do need (boy)," said (girl). "He can be the (tree) with the

honey. (boy) can hide and we can find him."

"But (boy) is too little to play," said Jane.

"I know (boy) is little," said (girl). "But he's my brother so he

can play, too."

(boy) was very happy to be a (tree) with honey.

Pooch, the Hero

New words for Pooch, the Hero

 monkey bars

 Father

 monkeys

Words you have learned

 Ethan

 tree

 Pooch

Pooch, the Hero

 and Scott are friends. They were playing in the park.

"Let's climb the 🪜," said 🧑.

"Woof," barked 🐕.

"🐕, you cannot climb 🪜," said Scott. 🧑 and Scott climbed

to the top of the 🪜. They pretended they were 🐒 in a 🌳.

🐕 sat at the bottom of the 🪜 and watched 🧑 and Scott.

"Let's climb down," said Scott.

🧑 and Scott looked down.

"I cannot climb down," said 🧑.

"Help," shouted Scott.

"Help. Help," yelled 🧑.

"Woof," barked 🐕. "Woof! Woof! Woof!" 🐕 ran around

the 🪜. Then he ran away.

"Come back, 🐕," called 🧑.

A little while later, 🐕 came back with 👨.

"🐕, you're our hero," said 🧑.

Doctor Jane

New words for Doctor Jane

 ball

 lollipop

 towel

Words you have learned

 Emmy

 hand

Doctor Jane

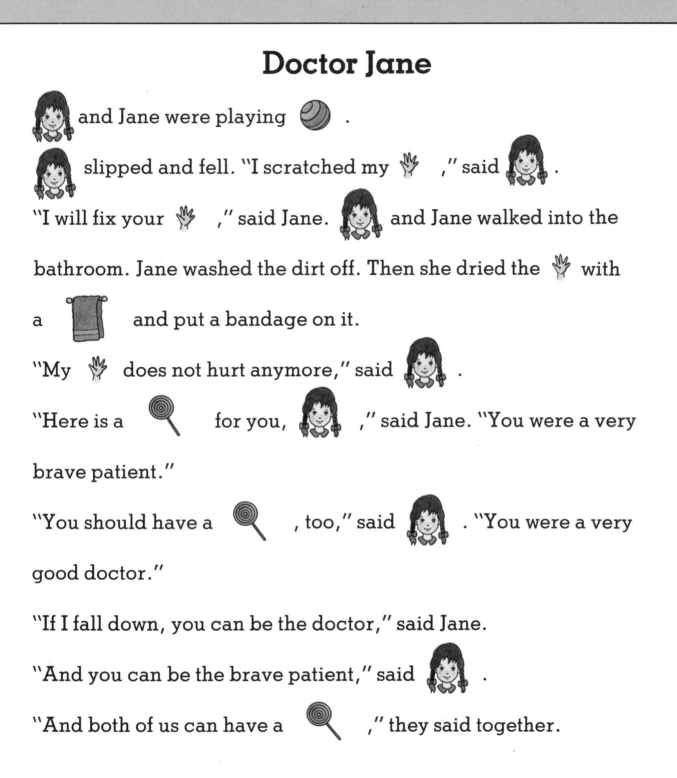

[girl] and Jane were playing [ball] .

[girl] slipped and fell. "I scratched my [hand] ," said [girl] .

"I will fix your [hand] ," said Jane. [girl] and Jane walked into the

bathroom. Jane washed the dirt off. Then she dried the [hand] with

a [towel] and put a bandage on it.

"My [hand] does not hurt anymore," said [girl] .

"Here is a [lollipop] for you, [girl] ," said Jane. "You were a very

brave patient."

"You should have a [lollipop] , too," said [girl] . "You were a very

good doctor."

"If I fall down, you can be the doctor," said Jane.

"And you can be the brave patient," said [girl] .

"And both of us can have a [lollipop] ," they said together.

Duck

Bear

Reading Books

MY FIRST COUNTING BOOK

3

SHAPES

S

ABC's

New words for Reading Books

school

books

bears

ducks

A A

B B

bone

dog

Words you have learned

Emmy

Ethan

tree

Reading Books

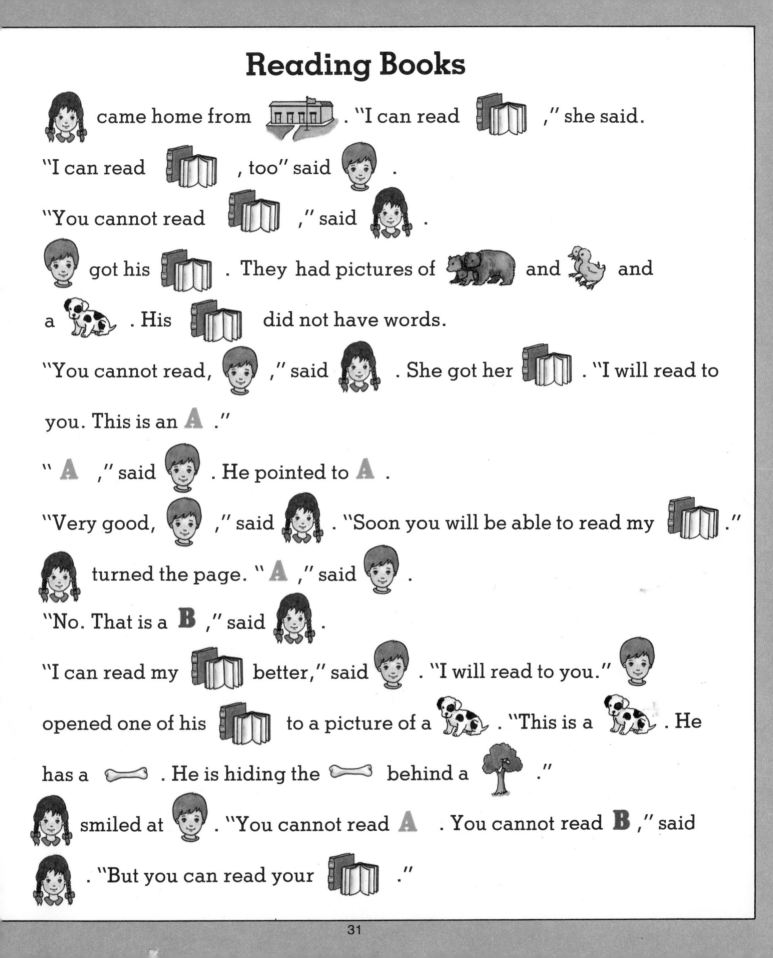

came home from 🏫 . "I can read 📖 ," she said.

"I can read 📖 , too" said 🧑 .

"You cannot read 📖 ," said 👧 .

🧑 got his 📖 . They had pictures of 🐻 and 🐥 and a 🐶 . His 📖 did not have words.

"You cannot read, 🧑 ," said 👧 . She got her 📖 . "I will read to you. This is an **A** ."

" **A** ," said 🧑 . He pointed to **A** .

"Very good, 🧑 ," said 👧 . "Soon you will be able to read my 📖 ."

👧 turned the page. " **A** ," said 🧑 .

"No. That is a **B** ," said 👧 .

"I can read my 📖 better," said 🧑 . "I will read to you." 🧑 opened one of his 📖 to a picture of a 🐶 . "This is a 🐶 . He has a 🦴 . He is hiding the 🦴 behind a 🌳 ."

👧 smiled at 🧑 . "You cannot read **A** . You cannot read **B** ," said 👧 . "But you can read your 📖 ."

Ethan's Birthday

New words for Ethan's Birthday

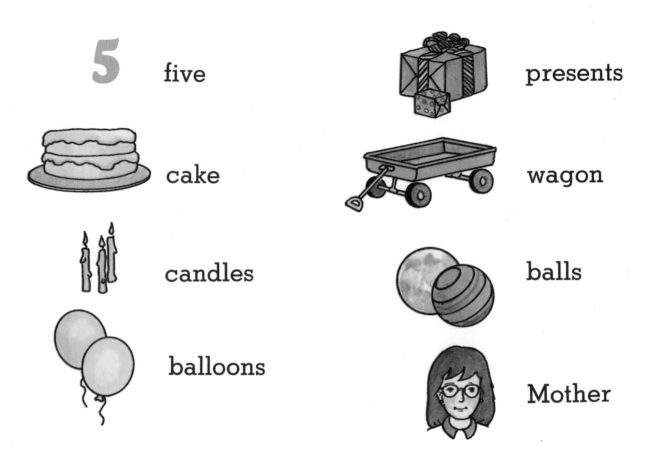

5 five

cake

candles

balloons

presents

wagon

balls

Mother

Words you have learned

Ethan

Emmy

 cars

Ethan's Birthday

[Ethan] was **5** years old today. At his birthday party, he had a [cake]

with [candles] . He had ice cream and [balloons] and [present] .

[Ethan] gave [girl] some [balloons] . She tied the [balloons] to her big

[wagon] .

"I want to ride in the [wagon] with the [balloons] ," said [Ethan] .

"You're too little," said [girl] . "You will fall out."

"It's time to open your [present] , [Ethan] ," said [mother] .

[Ethan] opened his [present] . He got [ball] and [car] . And [Ethan] got

a little [wagon] .

"Let me ride in your new [wagon] ," said [girl] .

"No," said [Ethan] . "You are too big. You will fall out."

"I will let you ride in my big [wagon] ," said [girl] .

"Okay," said [Ethan] . "Then I will let you ride in my little [wagon] ."

Rainy Day

New words for Rainy Day

window

dogs

crayons

cats

table

dinosaurs

bugs

Words you have learned

Mother

Emmy

Ethan

Rainy Day

Rain ran down the . "You have to play inside today," said . "Jane and Scott may come over to play, too."  put paper and  on the .  and  and Jane and Scott began to draw.

"I drew ," said .

"Me, too," said .

"No. These are ," said Jane.

"No. No. These are ," said Scott.

"," called . "Who drew ?"

 looked at the pictures. "There are a lot of different ," said . "Everyone drew ."

There are a lot of different ," said . "I am going to draw ."

There are a lot of different ," said Scott.

"And different ," said Jane.

 and  and Jane and Scott began to draw.

"Rainy days are fun," said .

"They sure are," agreed Scott,  and Jane.

Fun With Shapes

New words for Fun with Shapes

circle

cookie

wheel

square

book

block

rectangle

door

triangle

star

Words you have learned

Ethan

Mother

balls

table

Pooch

Fun With Shapes

and played a game.

"Here is a ○," said . "What is shaped like a ○, ?"

" are shaped like a ○," said . "So is a 🍪 and a ✳."

"Here is a ▢," said . "What is shaped like a ▢?"

"This Ⓐ is a ▢ and my ABC 📖, too," said .

"Here is an easy shape," said . "It is a ▭. What is shaped

like a ▭, ?"

The 🪑 is a ▭ and so is the 🚪," said .

"This is a △," said . "What is shaped like a △?"

"A △ is hard," said . He looked and looked. "I see a △.

The dog tag on 🐕 is a △."

"Woof," said 🐕 .

smiled at . "You get a ⭐ for the day," said .

Words You Have Learned in Little Kids at Play

Emmy	house
Ethan	bear
ice cream cone	tree
hand	monkey bars
Pooch	Father
cars	monkeys
blocks	ball
	towel
	lollipop
	school
	books
	bears
	ducks
	A
	B
	bone

dog

cake

candles

balloons

wagon

presents

Mother

balls

five   cookie

window   wheel

crayons   square

table   book

dinosaurs   block

dogs   rectangle

cats   door

bugs   triangle

circle   star